THE POWER OF ADAPTABILITY

DENISE SMITH

Copyright @ 2024 by Denise Smith

All rights reserved. No part of this book may be reproduced in any manner whatsoever without written permission except in the case of brief quotations embodied in critical articles and reviews.

First Edition, 2024

Table of Contents

Preface
  Foreword
  Emotional Regulation
  Emotional Intelligence
  Gratitude
  Perception
  Self-Awareness
  Sacrifice
  Confidence
  Persistence
  Self-Control
  Resilience
  Prioritization
  Setting Realistic Goals
  Time Management
  Table of Contents
  Organization
  Spiritual Warfare
  Mastering the Art of Detachment
  Accepting What you Cannot Control
  Legacy
  Change
  Complexion of Rejection
  A Letter to my Angel
  Acknowledgments
  Dedications

Preface

Adaptability: the quality of being able to adjust to new conditions and/or circumstances.

As a Single Mother of seven at the time of my jump into full entrepreneurship, I can truly say that the ability to adapt to everyday life and extenuating circumstances has been the driving force behind my success. From growing up without my father, being raised by a not so nurturing Mother, molested at the age of five, and looking for love in all the wrong places: I have certainly experienced my share of grief and despair.

Where I come from, you're lucky if you have a real shot at making it out of the projects.

Looking into the eyes of my children, I knew that there had to be more for us, and I wouldn't stop fighting until we had the chance to experience the life that we've always dreamed of. If I had to go out fighting and screaming then it's what I had to do. Either way, I understood that this was a fight that I would have to face with full force and by any means necessary in order to break the generational curses that had plagued my bloodline for many centuries.

It has been a treacherous journey to say the least. Hotel after hotel, shelter after shelter. No help in sight and left for dead at times. I knew that if I did not learn to adapt, life would swallow me whole and my children would reap the consequences.

Even to this day, I continue to fight! Using the principles that I have presented to you to strategically maneuver through life.

Setting realistic goals and tackling them one by one. Walking boldly, confidently and fiercely in all that God has called me to do and be. I now understand that anything that I am not changing I am ultimately choosing.

I continue to put my life on the line because the power behind my legacy is so much bigger than me.

Recognizing the significant power of adaptability has single-handedly changed my life and it has the power to create an avenue for anyone to become almost anything that they desire to be.

If I can do it, so can you!

-Denise Smith
The Power of Adaptability- Alpha Science

FOREWORD

We learn to adapt by accepting Gods plans for our lives. We have this idea of what life is supposed to look like for us. When what we should be doing is praying for strength and guidance to conquer whatever life may decide to throw at us.

On a scale of one to ten, how well would you say you are prepared to deal with the effects of a major life shift or anything else that would cause a mental breakdown? Well, maybe I can be of assistance.

This book consists of twenty important principles to help you Master the Power of Adaptability the Alpha Way!

THE POWER OF ADAPTABILITY

1

Chapter 1: Emotional Regulation

Emotional Regulation is the ability to take control over one's own emotional state.

Differentiating between negative and positive thoughts and emotions.

Processing all thoughts as positive thoughts even if they are negative.

Taking time to process your emotions.

Setting boundaries with yourself and others.

Distancing yourself from negative energies and frequencies.

Thinking before speaking.

Implementing breathing techniques.

Considering all perspectives.

Differentiating between negative and positive emotions is the first step to emotional regulation. Most times we act out of emotion because we have not taken the proper time to process certain emotions.

Being in toxic environments too long can also cloud one's judgement while under the pressure or facing certain circumstances.

Separating the natural from the spiritual is vital. Since we are spiritual beings, it is important to understand that our bodies in its entirety is only the physical manifestation of fulfilling our God-given purpose.

The mind is a natural part of us that has been programmed by those other than a higher power until we gain control of our subconscious.

Whether it be religion, our parents or the environments we were in.

It is our job as adults to work toward unlearning toxic and negative behaviors and/or emotions.

That means reprogramming and disciplining ourselves to hear from God and respond to things in a manner that exemplifies our character in a positive manner.

It doesn't happen overnight, but working toward emotional regulation is a non-negotiable in reference to mastering adaptability.

Emotional regulation refers to the ability to manage and respond to an emotional experience in a healthy and balanced way. It's a crucial skill that helps individuals handle stress, interact positively with others, and make thoughtful decisions. Why is Emotional Regulation Important?

Proper emotional regulation can reduce symptoms of anxiety and depression. It improves communication and cooperation with others. It aids in making more rational and less impulsive decisions. It also aids in coping with stressful situations more effectively.

Some strategies for Emotional Regulation include....

Mindfulness:

Practicing mindfulness can increase awareness of your emotional state without immediately reacting to it. Techniques include meditation, deep breathing, and grounding exercises.

Cognitive Reappraisal:

This involves changing the way you think about a situation to alter its emotional impact.

Expressive Writing:

Writing about your emotions can help you better process them. This can involve keeping a journal or simply jotting down your feelings on paper.

Physical Activity:

Exercise can be a great way to manage emotions. Activities like jogging, yoga, or even going for a walk can help reduce stress and improve your mood.

Social Support:

Talking to friends, family, or a therapist that you trust can provide a different perspective and emotional relief.

Healthy Habits:

Maintaining a balanced diet, getting enough sleep, and avoiding excessive use of alcohol or drugs can also improve your ability to regulate emotions.

Recognizing Emotional Triggers:

Understanding what triggers your emotions is the first step in managing them. Keep track of situations that cause strong emotional responses and reflect on why they affect you. Over time, this awareness can help you anticipate and prepare for emotional challenges.

Practicing Patience and Self-Compassion:

It's important to be patient with yourself as you work on improving your emotional regulation. Everyone has moments when their emotions get the best of them.

Practicing self-compassion means treating yourself with the same kindness and understanding that you would offer to a friend.

In conclusion, emotional regulation is not about suppressing your feelings but rather managing them in a way that is beneficial to your overall well-being. By practicing various strategies and being mindful of your emotional triggers, you can improve your emotional health and lead a more balanced life.

2

Chapter 2: Emotional Intelligence

Emotional Intelligence is the ability to understand and manage both your own emotions and the emotions of others. This can look like....

Practicing self-awareness.
Implementing emotional regulation.
Motivating yourself and others.
Displaying empathy toward yourself and others.
Successfully managing difficult situations.
Expressing yourself clearly.
Listening to understand not to respond.
Relaying responses that follow understanding.

Emotional intelligence gives healthy, whole and healed vibes. The ability to connect with others in a way that is calm, peaceful and intellectual is a sure way to set you apart from your counterparts.

As for me, intellectual conversation will win me over every time.

To have an intellectual conversation with another you need to work toward emotional intelligence. Those who are emotionally intelligent aren't blinded by only their own perspectives and perceptions.

They have the ability to recognize the point of view of another without bias and the interjection of their own viewpoints.

Emotional intelligence is the foreplay of two people compromising different perspectives, opinions and point of views to come to a positive disposition. Even if the disposition is agreeing to disagree.

The compromise is one of the greatest components to a strong foundation of communication in friendships, romantic relationships and business relationships.

Compromise represents love, respect, empathy.

Emotional intelligence refers to the ability to recognize, understand, manage, and effectively use emotions in ourselves and others.

It's a crucial skill that can enhance personal and professional relationships, improve communication, and foster a more harmonious and productive environment.

Some key components of emotional intelligence are...

Self-Awareness:

This is the foundation of emotional intelligence. It involves being aware of your own emotions and how they affect your thoughts and behaviors. Self-awareness allows you to understand your strengths and weaknesses and recognize how your emotions influence your interactions with others.

Self-Regulation:

Once you are aware of your emotions, the next step is to manage them effectively. Self-regulation involves controlling impulsive feelings and behaviors, managing your emotions in healthy ways, and taking responsibility for your actions.

Motivation:

Emotionally intelligent individuals are often driven by an inner ambition and a passion for their work. They set goals, remain committed, and are resilient in the face of challenges.

Empathy:

This involves understanding and sharing the feelings of others. Empathy allows you to connect with people on a deeper level, build stronger relationships, and respond to others' needs and concerns more effectively.

Social Skills:

These include the ability to communicate clearly, manage conflicts, build strong relationships, and work well in teams. Good social skills are essential for effective leadership, collaborations, and partnerships.

Tips for Developing Emotional Intelligence

Reflect on Your Emotions:

Take time each day to reflect on your emotions and what triggered them. Keeping a journal can help you track patterns and gain insights into your emotional responses.

Practice Mindfulness:

Mindfulness techniques, such as meditation, can help you become more aware of your emotions and stay present in the moment. This can improve your ability to manage stress and respond to situations calmly.

Develop Active Listening Skills:

Practice active listening by paying full attention to the speaker, observing their body language, and responding thoughtfully. This shows empathy and helps build stronger connections.

Seek Feedback:

Ask for feedback from friends, family, or colleagues that you trust about how you handle your emotions and interactions. Constructive feedback can provide valuable insights and help you improve.

Manage Stress:

Learn and implement stress management techniques such as deep breathing, exercise, or hobbies. Managing stress effectively can help you maintain emotional balance and respond more positively to challenging situations.

Work on Conflict Resolution:

Learn how to handle conflicts constructively by staying calm, listening to all parties involved, and finding mutually beneficial solutions. Effective conflict resolution is a key aspect of social skills.

Practice Empathy:

Put yourself in others' shoes and try to understand their perspectives and feelings. This can enhance your ability to connect with others and respond to their needs. Developing emotional intelligence is a lifelong journey, but the benefits are well worth the effort. By enhancing your emotional intelligence you can improve your relationships, achieve greater personal and professional success, and contribute to a more positive and understanding world.

3

Chapter 3: Gratitude

Gratitude is the quality of being thankful; a readiness to show appreciation for and to return kindness. This could mirror....
Showing appreciation toward yourself or another.
Reflecting on good things that are happening to and for you.
Being thankful for the things that people often take for granted.
Ex. Life, a place to live, food, clean water, family and friends.
Expressing gratitude.
Implying gratitude.
Fostering Resilience.
Detering from negativity
Posturing yourself for abundance.
Starting your day with gratitude.
Having the ability to change the temperature in the room.
Deciding to live everyday as your last day.
Gratitude is essentially the key principle to abundance.
Without expressing gratitude there's no room for God to bless us with more.
Most people on focus on practicing gratitude only during the thanksgiving holiday. When we should be practicing gratitude every single day.

Whether it's something that you do quietly to yourself or around a table with loved ones, expressing gratitude is something that we all should implement into our daily routines.

Studies also show that expressing gratitude has many health benefits and can lead to a person's happiness on a larger scale.

Practicing even the smallest amount of gratitude can have such a large impact on your life.

Gratitude is about grounding yourself and focusing on the good. The good can be anything that makes you happy: from the cup of coffee that you had this morning to the people who are a part of your life.

Practicing gratitude is not lecturing yourself and saying, "you should be grateful." Or, "other people have it worse."

Instead, it's about spending time to focus, reflect, and meditate on the good, however large or small that may be. By regularly taking some time to do so, you will develop habits (and even rewire your brain!) to think and live a little more positively, benefitting both your mental and physical health.

We all need more sleep! People who practice gratitude before bed are proven to sleep better. It totally makes sense! We all know that spiral of negativity that keeps so many of us awake.

By regularly practicing gratitude, you're more likely to be able to focus on positive thoughts at bedtime and avoid that negative self-talk that keeps us awake.

We live in a society of judgment, competition, and unreachable standards that tries to crush our self-esteem, resulting in negative and unhealthy relationships to our bodies and selves. Practicing gratitude is a great way to combat negative self-talk and feeling less than. Rather than compare ourselves to others (whether it be physically, emotionally, career, etc.) gratitude helps us to center ourselves and focus on the positives, improving our overall outlook on life and ourselves!

It sounds obvious, but it's true. By routinely practicing gratitude, you rewire your brain to think more positively. Gratitude literally makes you produce "happy hormones" aka dopamine and serotonin.

Just like with physical exercise; by regularly practicing gratitude, you can literally strengthen these neural pathways, resulting in better and long-lasting production of positive feelings.

This is certainly not suggesting this is a cure for depression or anxiety, but it truly does make a difference on your mental health by regularly taking time to focus on positives.

4

Chapter 4: Perception

Perception is a way of regarding, understanding, or interpreting something; a mental impression.

The way in which we mentally receive and process information is imperative to our personal, mental, emotional, physical, spiritual and financial growth. Understanding that everything and everyone that we encounter can either have a positive or negative impact on our lives with the determining factor being how we perceive things.

Perception is the process by which individuals organize and interpret their sensory impressions to give meaning to their environment. It involves the brain taking in information from the five senses of sight, hearing, taste, touch, and smell—and making sense of it.

Key Aspects of Perception are.....
What we see with our eyes.
What we hear with our ears.
What we smell with our nose.
What we taste with our tongue.
What we feel through our skin.

We cannot process all sensory information at once. Attention will always act as a filter, allowing us to focus on certain stimuli while ignoring the others.

Interpretation: Our brains interpret sensory information based on past experiences, knowledge, and expectations. This interpretation can be influenced by cultural and social contexts.

Organization: Perception involves organizing sensory input into a coherent whole. For example, we might see individual leaves, but we perceive them together as a tree.

Perceptual Set: This refers to a predisposition to perceive things in a certain way, often influenced by our expectations, motives, and emotions.

Perception is crucial for survival; it helps us detect danger, find food, and navigate our environment.

Communication enables us to understand and respond to others, facilitating social interactions and relationships.

Perception influences our judgments and decisions by providing the necessary information to evaluate our surroundings.

Age, health, and sensory impairments can also affect perception.

Emotions, motives, and experiences play a significant role in how we perceive the world.

Cultural background can shape the way we interpret sensory information and the meanings we assign to it.

Perception is a complex but fascinating process that allows us to make sense of our world. By understanding how perception works and the factors that influence it, we can better appreciate the rich tapestry of human experience and communication.

Chapter 5: Self-Awareness

Self-Awareness is the ability to understand yourself, including your thoughts, feelings, values, beliefs, and actions. It also means being able to recognize how others see you, and to acknowledge your strengths and weaknesses.

Your ability to perceive and understand the things that make you who you are as an individual, including your personality, actions, values, beliefs, and emotions.

Self-awareness is the conscious knowledge of your own character, feelings, motives, and desires. It's a fundamental aspect of personal development and emotional intelligence. Being self-aware allows you to understand your strengths and weaknesses, recognize your emotional triggers, and comprehend how your actions impact others.

Developing self-awareness can happen through various methods such as reflection, mindfulness, and seeking feedback from others. Reflection involves taking time to think about your actions, thoughts, and feelings. This can be done through journaling or meditative practices. Mindfulness focuses on being present in the moment and observing your thoughts and feelings without judgment. Seeking feedback from others involves asking trusted friends, family, or colleagues that you trust for their perspective on your behavior and attitudes.

Self-awareness contributes to better decision-making, improved relationships, and greater overall well-being. It allows people to align their actions with their values, leading to a more fulfilling and authentic life. By understanding and accepting who you are, you can work towards becoming the person you want to be.

Self-awareness is a crucial aspect of personal development and emotional intelligence. It involves having a clear understanding of your own thoughts, emotions, strengths, weaknesses, and behaviors. Here are some key points to consider when exploring the concept of self-awareness:

Importance of Self-Awareness

Improved Emotional Intelligence:

Being self-aware helps you recognize your emotional responses and manage them effectively. This is essential for maintaining healthy relationships and making informed decisions.

Better Decision Making:

Understanding your motivations and values allows you to make choices that align with your true self, leading to greater satisfaction and fulfillment.

Enhanced Relationships:

When you are aware of your own behaviors and how they affect others, you can communicate more effectively and build stronger, more meaningful connections.

Personal Growth:

Self-awareness is the first step in personal development. It allows you to identify areas for improvement and set realistic goals for growth.

Ways to Cultivate Self-Awareness

Reflection:

Spend time reflecting on your experiences and how they have shaped your beliefs and behaviors.

Mindfulness:

Practice mindfulness techniques, such as meditation, to become more aware of your thoughts and feelings in the present moment.

Seek Feedback:

Ask for feedback from trusted friends, family, or colleagues that you trust. They can provide valuable insights into how you are perceived and how your actions impact others.

Establishing A Personal Relationship with God:

A personal relationship with God can have many benefits including forgiveness, divine strength, perfect peace, knowing you're loved and have a purpose, recognizing your identity, living free from fear, receiving guidance and practicing gratitude.

Seek Professional Help:

Consider working with a coach or therapist that you trust who can help you explore your inner world and develop greater self-awareness.

Challenges of Self-Awareness

Facing Uncomfortable Truths:

Becoming self-aware often requires confronting aspects of yourself that you may prefer to ignore. This can be challenging but is essential for growth.

Consistency:

Maintaining self-awareness is an ongoing process that requires continual effort and reflection.

Balancing Self-Perception:

It's important to balance self-awareness with self-acceptance. While it's crucial to recognize areas for improvement, it's equally important to acknowledge and celebrate your strengths.

Developing self-awareness is a powerful tool for achieving personal growth and improving your interactions with the world around you. By taking the time to understand yourself better, you can lead a more intentional, fulfilling life.

6

Chapter 6: Sacrifice

Sacrifice is often a requirement for success in entrepreneurship, especially in the early stages of a startup. Entrepreneurs may need to give up many things to achieve their goals, including:

Relationships: Entrepreneurs may sacrifice relationships with friends, family, or significant others.

Health: Entrepreneurs may experience stress and uncertainty, which can negatively impact their health.

Income and standard of living: Entrepreneurs may need to sacrifice their previous income and standards of living. This often looks like living way below your means in an attempt to pour into your entrepreneurial journey and vision.

Stability: Entrepreneurs may sacrifice stability and security as they branch out into full entrepreneurship.

Work-life balance: Entrepreneurs may need to sacrifice their work-life balance.

Control: Entrepreneurs may need to sacrifice control in several different aspects.

Sacrifice is a concept that permeates many aspects of life, from personal relationships to professional endeavors, and even cultural and religious practices. At its core, sacrifice involves giving up something of value for the sake of something else that is considered more important or worthy in the latter. This act often requires a significant level of commitment, selflessness, and foresight.

In personal relationships, sacrifice can take many forms. Parents might sacrifice their time and resources to ensure their children have a better future. Friends may sacrifice their own comfort to support each other during tough times. In romantic relationships, partners often make sacrifices to maintain harmony and ensure the relationship thrives.

Professionally, sacrifice can be seen in the dedication individuals demonstrate towards their careers. This might involve working long hours, pursuing further education, or even relocating to seize better opportunities.

The sacrifices made in one's career can lead to personal growth and professional success, but they often require balancing other aspects of life, such as family and personal well-being.

In cultural and religious contexts, sacrifice often has a deep symbolic meaning. Many cultures and religions have rituals or traditions that involve some form of sacrifice, whether it be through offerings, fasting, or other acts of devotion.

These sacrifices are typically made to honor deities, seek blessings, or show gratitude and commitment to your faith.

Ultimately, the concept of sacrifice is intertwined with the values and priorities of individuals and societies. While the act of sacrificing can be challenging and demanding, it is often seen as a noble and necessary endeavor that contributes to personal fulfillment and the greater good.

7

Chapter 7: Confidence

Confidence is the state of feeling certain about the truth of something.

A feeling of self-assurance arising from one's appreciation of one's own abilities or qualities.

Confidence is the belief in one's abilities and judgment. It's a crucial quality that can significantly impact various aspects of life, from personal relationships to professional success. Confident people tend to approach challenges with a positive mindset, are more likely to take risks, and often inspire others around them.

Building confidence involves several steps:

Self-Awareness: Understanding your strengths and weaknesses can help you set realistic goals and recognize areas for improvement.

Positive Thinking: Focus on your achievements and positive traits. This can counteract negative thoughts that undermine confidence.

Practice and Preparation: Whether it's public speaking or a job interview, practicing can reduce anxiety and increase your confidence in your abilities.

Learning from Failure: Instead of viewing failure as a setback, see it as an opportunity to learn and grow. Every mistake is a stepping stone to success.

Surrounding Yourself with Supportive People: Being around positive and encouraging individuals can boost your self-esteem and confidence.

Confidence is not about being perfect; it's about trusting yourself and your capabilities while being open to growth and new experiences. Confidence is a journey, not a destination.

8

Chapter 8: Persistence

Persistence is the quality that allows someone to continue doing something or trying to do something even though it is difficult or opposed by other people.

Persistence is a trait that is often praised and sought after in various aspects of life, from personal goals to professional achievements. It refers to the ability to continue steadfastly in a course of action, despite facing adversity, difficulties, obstacles, or discouragement. This quality can be the difference between achieving success and giving up prematurely.

One of the most notable aspects of persistence is its role in personal growth and development. When we set goals for ourselves, whether they are related to education, business, fitness, personal relationships or hobbies, it is persistence that keeps us moving forward, even when progress seems slow or setbacks occur.

For example, learning a new skill, such as playing a musical instrument or mastering a foreign language, often requires sustained effort and practice over an extended period. Those who persist are more likely to reach a level of proficiency that brings them satisfaction and fulfillment.

In the professional realm, persistence is equally important. Many successful individuals and innovators attribute their achievements to their unwavering commitment to their goals and/or careers.

I have failed many times and taken many losses. But I have never quit.

Persistence is not just about sheer willpower; it also involves adaptability and resilience. It means being willing to adjust your approach when necessary, learning from failures, and not being afraid to try again.

This adaptability piece is crucial because it allows us to navigate changing circumstances and find new solutions to our problems.

Persistence can also have a positive impact on mental health and well-being. It fosters a sense of purpose and direction, which can be motivating and fulfilling.

Overcoming challenges through persistent effort can boost self-esteem and confidence, reinforcing the belief that one is capable of achieving their biggest dreams and aspirations.

Persistence is a vital quality that empowers individuals to pursue and attain their goals despite obstacles. It involves a combination of determination, adaptability, and resilience, all of which contribute to personal and professional success.

By cultivating persistence, we can navigate life's challenges more effectively and achieve a greater sense of accomplishment and satisfaction.

9

Chapter 9: Dependability

Dependability is the quality of being trustworthy and reliable. Dependability is a critical trait that encompasses reliability, consistency, and trustworthiness. It is the foundation upon which strong relationships, both personal and professional, are built. When someone is dependable, they follow through on their commitments and can be counted on to deliver results.

Even in entrepreneurship, dependability means showing up on time, meeting deadlines, and maintaining a high standard of work ethic. It fosters a sense of trust among colleagues and partnerships, creating a more productive and positive environment.

Dependable entrepreneurs often gain more opportunities for advancement because they prove they can be relied upon.

In personal relationships, dependability is equally important. It means being there for friends and family when they need support, keeping promises, and being consistent in your actions and behavior. This reliability strengthens bonds and builds a sense of security and trust.

Overall, dependability is a fundamental quality that enhances one's reputation and fosters lasting, meaningful connections.

It is a trait that is highly valued and respected in all areas of life.

Dependability is a critical trait that underpins trust and reliability in both personal and professional relationships. It involves consistently fulfilling obligations, being punctual, and maintaining a level of responsibility in various situations. When someone is dependable, others can count on them to do what they say they will do, which fosters a sense of security and predictability.

In the entrepreneurship, dependability translates to meeting deadlines, delivering quality work, and supporting colleagues. Others highly value this trait as it contributes to a stable and productive environment. For instance, a dependable entrepreneur consistently shows up on time, completes tasks efficiently, and can be trusted to handle responsibilities without constant supervision.

In personal relationships, dependability is equally important. It means being there for friends and family when needed, keeping promises, and being a steady presence during both good times and bad. This builds strong, lasting bonds and ensures that relationships are built on a foundation of trust.

Developing dependability involves cultivating good habits such as time management, clear communication, and follow-throughs. It also means being honest about your capabilities and not overcommitting yourself. By doing so, you not only enhance your own reputation but also contribute positively to the environments you are part of.

Being dependable is a highly valued trait in both personal and professional settings. It means that others can rely on you to follow through with your commitments, meet deadlines, and be consistent in your actions. Dependability builds trust and strengthens relationships, making it an essential quality for success and collaboration.

To be dependable, start by setting realistic expectations for yourself and others. Understand your limits and communicate them clearly. If you promise something, ensure you have the capability and resources to deliver. Consistency is key; regularly meeting your commitments will create a track record of reliability.

Time management plays a crucial role in dependability. Prioritize your tasks and manage your time effectively to avoid last-minute rushes and missed deadlines. Use tools like calendars, planners, or task management apps to stay organized and keep track of your obligations.

Another important aspect is accountability. Own up to your mistakes and learn from them. If unforeseen circumstances prevent you from fulfilling a promise, communicate proactively and offer solutions or alternatives. This shows that you are responsible and committed to maintaining trust.

Being dependable also involves being present and attentive. Whether it's showing up on time for meetings, being responsive to communication, or providing support when needed, your presence and engagement demonstrate that you value others' time and trust.

In essence, being dependable is about consistency, reliability, and accountability. It fosters trust and respect, paving the way for stronger, more productive relationships both personally and professionally.

10

Chapter 10: Self-Control

Self-control is a crucial skill that enables us to regulate our emotions, thoughts, and behaviors in the face of temptations and impulses. It is essential for achieving personal goals, maintaining healthy relationships, and leading a balanced life.

Some key aspects of self-control are.....

Personal Achievement: Self-control helps in setting and reaching personal goals, whether they are academic, professional, or related to personal well-being. It involves delaying gratification and staying focused on long-term objectives.

Healthy Relationships: Managing our emotions and reactions can prevent conflicts and misunderstandings, fostering better communication and stronger bonds with others.

Mental Health: Practicing self-control can reduce stress and anxiety by providing a sense of control over our lives. It also helps in avoiding impulsive decisions that could lead to negative consequences.

Some strategies to improving self-control are.....

Goal Setting: Clearly define your goals and break them down into manageable steps. This makes them less overwhelming and much easier to achieve.

Mindfulness and Meditation: These practices increase awareness of your thoughts and feelings, helping you to stay calm and focused.

Healthy Habits: Regular exercise, a balanced diet, and adequate sleep can improve your overall ability to exert self-control.

Avoiding Temptation: Creating an environment that minimizes temptations can make it easier to stay on track.

Positive Reinforcement: Reward yourself for small victories along the way. This can help maintain motivation and reinforce positive production.

In conclusion, self-control is a vital skill that can significantly enhance the quality of your life. By understanding its importance and implementing strategies to strengthen it, you can navigate challenges more effectively and achieve your personal and professional aspirations.

11

Chapter 11: Prioritization

Prioritization is the action or process of deciding the relative importance or urgency of a thing or things.

Prioritization is the process of arranging tasks or items in order of importance or urgency. It's a crucial skill in both personal and professional settings, enabling us to manage our time effectively, meet deadlines, and achieve our goals. Here are some steps to prioritizing your goals.

Identify Your Goals

Short-term Goals:
These are tasks or objectives you aim to achieve in the near future.

Long-term Goals:
These are broader objectives that take more time to accomplish.

Categorize Tasks
Urgent vs. Important:
    Categorize tasks into four quadrants:
    Urgent and Important
Important but Not Urgent

Urgent but Not Important
Neither Urgent nor Important

Focus on tasks in the first two categories to make sure you're handling critical responsibilities effectively.

By systematically working through tasks, you're more likely to achieve both short-term and long-term goals.

In conclusion, prioritization is a dynamic and ongoing process that requires regular assessment and adjustment.

By implementing these strategies, you can manage your goals more effectively, reduce stress, and enhance your overall productivity.

12

Chapter 12: Setting Realistic Goals

Realistic goals are attainable given your skills, motivation, and time frame. They can help you make progress, spark excitement, and drive you to learn new skills.

Some tips for setting realistic goals:

Use the SMART method

SMART is an acronym that stands for Specific, Measurable, Achievable, Relevant, and Time-bound.

Consider your resources and threats

Make sure you have the resources you need to achieve your goal, and consider any potential obstacles.

Set milestones

Break your goals down into smaller steps and create a timeline for completing them.

Be flexible

Keep your goals reviewable so you can adjust them if needed.

Believe in your goals

If you don't believe in your goals from the start, it's hard to consider them realistic.

Setting realistic goals is essential for achieving success and maintaining motivation.

Here are some key steps to help you set and achieve realistic goals:

Define Your Objectives Clearly
Specific: Clearly define what you want to achieve. Instead of setting a vague goal like "get fit," specify "lose 10 pounds in 3 months" or "run a 5K in 8 weeks."

Measurable: Ensure your goal can be quantified or measured. This helps in tracking progress and staying motivated.

Achievable: Set goals that are challenging but attainable. Consider your current abilities and resources.

Relevant: Align your goals with your broader life objectives and values.

Time-bound: Set a deadline for your goal. Having a timeline creates a sense of urgency and helps with planning.

Break Down Goals Into Manageable Steps

• Action Plan: Create a step-by-step plan detailing how you'll achieve each short-term goal. This makes the process less overwhelming.

Monitor Your Progress
Regular Check-ins: Regularly review your progress to see if you are on track. Adjust your plan if necessary.

Celebrate Milestones: Recognize and celebrate small successes along the way to stay motivated.

Stay Flexible

• Adjust as Needed: Life is unpredictable. Be prepared to adjust your goals and plans as circumstances change.

- Learn from Setbacks: Treat obstacles and failures as learning opportunities rather than reasons to give up.

    Seek Support and Accountability

- Share Your Goals: Tell friends, family, or colleagues that you trust about your goals. Their support and encouragement can be invaluable.
    - Find an Accountability Partner: Having someone to check in with can help you stay committed and motivated.

    Stay Positive and Persistent
- Positive Mindset: Maintain a positive attitude and believe in your ability to achieve your goals.

- Persistence: Stay committed, even when progress seems to be stagnated.

    Consistency is the key to achieving long-term goals.

By following these steps, you can set realistic goals that are achievable and maintainable, leading to greater satisfaction and success in your endeavors.

Chapter 13: Time Management

Time management is the coordination of tasks and activities to maximize the effectiveness of an individual's efforts.

Essentially, the purpose of time management is to enable people to get more and better work done in less time.

Elements of time management include organization, planning and scheduling to best take advantage of the time available. Time management techniques also take into account an individual's particular situation and their relevant capabilities and characteristics.

Why is time management important?

The importance of time management is in its ability to assign meaning to time, letting people make the most of their time. In a business context, it is used to set goals and expectations. Good time management skills help employees deliver quality work and meet their goals effectively. Time management also helps to understand what you are capable of and to set realistic goals.

Poor time management skills cause you to miss goals and deliver poor work, become overly stressed out and anxious, and run short of time. When time is used inefficiently, it has deleterious effects on your mental capacity.

Time poverty is a result of poor or nonexistent time management. People find themselves in this state when they have too much to do and too little time to do it. Their personal lives suffer, and they feel increasingly overwhelmed with responsibilities and activities despite working hard.

Time management requires active decisions about what you want and need to do. Without time management, you continually react to external stimuli and lose a sense of control over your work and life.

All work takes time, but some tasks are more valuable than others. Reallocating time to higher-value work improves both productivity and work-life balance. Good time management creates a healthier work space overall.

The benefits of effective time management apply equally to business and entrepreneurship. Some of these benefits include the following:

Happier Vibes. When you have enough time to get your work done, you are happier and less prone to burnout.

Improved creativity. When not stressed by time issues, you have the space and energy to be more creative in your work. You can actively engage with your work instead of passively reacting to it. This increases innovation.

Lower absenteeism. Stressed and burned-out entrepreneurs take more sick and other time off.

Lower turnover. With a better work experience, you are more likely to meet deadlines.

Increased productivity. Entrepreneurs who are less likely to be burned out and who enjoy their work are more productive.

Enhanced reputation. Entrepreneurs that encourage effective time management are known as great people to work with, improving recruitment and retention.

Time management is a crucial skill that can significantly improve your productivity, reduce stress, and help you achieve your goals more efficiently. Here are some key strategies to master time management:

Prioritize Tasks

Set SMART Goals
- Specific: Clearly define what you want to achieve.
- Measurable: Ensure you can track your progress.
- Achievable: Set realistic goals.
- Relevant: Align goals with your broader objectives.
- Time-bound: Set a deadline.

Use a Planner or Digital Tools
- Physical Planners: Write down tasks, deadlines, and appointments.
- Digital Tools: Utilize apps like Google Calendar, Trello, or Asana to keep track of your schedule and tasks.

Break Tasks into Smaller Steps
- Micro-Tasks: Divide larger tasks into manageable steps to avoid feeling overwhelmed.
- Pomodoro Technique: Work for 25 minutes, then take a 5-minute break. Repeat the cycle to maintain focus.

Avoid Procrastination
- Set Deadlines: Even for small tasks, set a clear deadline.
- Eliminate Distractions: Identify and remove distractions from your work environment.

Delegate When Possible
- Identify Tasks to Delegate: Determine which tasks can be handled by others.
- Communicate Clearly: Provide clear instructions and expectations when delegating.

Review and Reflect
- Daily Review: At the end of each day, review what you've accomplished and plan for the next day.

- Weekly Reflection: Reflect on your achievements and areas for improvement each week.

Balance Work and Personal Life
- Set Boundaries: Clearly separate work time from personal time.
- Schedule Downtime: Ensure you have time for relaxation and hobbies.

Learn to Say No
- Assess Requests: Before committing to new tasks, evaluate if they align with your priorities.
- Polite Decline: If a request doesn't fit your schedule or goals, politely decline.

Continuous Improvement
- Seek Feedback: Ask for feedback on your time management from peers or mentors that you trust.
- Adapt Strategies: Be open to changing and adapting your time management strategies as needed.

By implementing these strategies, you can enhance your efficiency, reduce stress, and achieve a better balance between your personal and professional life.

Chapter 14: Organization

Organization is the action of organizing something.
Organization is a fundamental skill that impacts numerous aspects of life, from personal productivity to professional success. At its core, organization involves arranging and managing tasks, resources, and time in an efficient manner to achieve specific goals.

Below are key elements and tips for maintaining effective organization:

• Prioritize Tasks: Use methods to categorize tasks based on their urgency and importance.

• Set Deadlines: Establish clear deadlines for each task to ensure timely completion and avoid procrastination.

• Use a Calendar: Digital or physical calendars can help keep track of important dates, meetings, and deadlines.

Effective organization can lead to improved productivity, reduced stress, and a greater sense of control over your life. By implementing these strategies, you can create a more structured and efficient approach to managing your tasks and responsibilities.

Chapter 15: Spiritual Warfare

Spiritual warfare is a Christian concept that involves fighting against evil forces that are said to interfere in human affairs. It's based on the biblical belief in demons or evil spirits.

Spiritual warfare is a concept found in many religious traditions that refers to the struggle between good and evil forces. In Christianity, spiritual warfare often involves the belief that there are unseen battles between angels and demons, with humans caught in the middle. This struggle is thought to affect individuals on a personal level, influencing their thoughts, actions, and spiritual well-being.

Key Concepts in Spiritual Warfare

The Enemy:

In Christian theology, the enemy often refers to Satan and his demons. These forces are believed to work against God and His followers, attempting to lead people into sin and away from the path of righteousness.

Armor of God:

Ephesians 6:10-18 describes the "Armor of God," a metaphor for the spiritual tools believers can use to protect themselves. This includes the belt of truth, breastplate of righteousness, shield of faith, helmet of salvation, and sword of the Spirit (the Word of God).

Prayer and Fasting:
These are considered powerful weapons in spiritual warfare. Prayer is a way to communicate with God, seek His guidance, and ask for His protection. Fasting is often used to deepen one's spiritual focus and discipline.

Scripture:
The Bible is seen as a crucial resource for understanding and combating spiritual attacks. Believers are encouraged to read, memorize, and meditate on Scripture to strengthen their faith and resilience.

Discernment:
This involves the ability to distinguish between good and evil influences. It is considered essential for recognizing spiritual attacks and responding appropriately.

How to Fight Against Spiritual Warfare

Stay Grounded in Faith:
Regular worship, Bible study, and fellowship with other believers can help strengthen your faith and keep you grounded.

Try To Live Righteously:
Strive to live according to the teachings of your faith. Leading a moral and ethical life can make you less susceptible to negative influences.

Pray Regularly:
Maintain a consistent prayer life. Prayer can provide guidance, protection, and strength in times of spiritual struggle.

Use Scripture:

Familiarize yourself with key Bible verses that address spiritual warfare. Recite them in times of need to remind yourself of God's promises and power.

Seek Support:

Don't hesitate to reach out to spiritual leaders or fellow believers that you trust for support and guidance. Community can be a strong ally in spiritual battles.

Spiritual warfare is a deeply personal and often complex aspect of faith. For those who believe, it involves a constant vigilance and reliance on spiritual practices to navigate the challenges posed by unseen forces. While the concept may differ across various religions, the common thread is the struggle for spiritual integrity and the pursuit of a righteous life.

16

Chapter 16: Mastering the Art of Detachment

Mastering the art of detachment is a valuable skill that can significantly improve your emotional well-being and overall quality of life. Detachment doesn't mean becoming indifferent or uncaring; rather, it's about maintaining healthy boundaries and not letting external factors control your inner peace.

Here are some key steps to help you master the art of detachment:

Understand the Concept of Detachment
Detachment is about separating your emotions and self-worth from the outcomes of situations and the actions of others. It's recognizing that you can't control everything and learning to live in the present moment without becoming overly attached to specific outcomes.

Practice Mindfulness
Mindfulness involves being present in the moment and observing your thoughts and feelings without judgment. This practice can help you become more aware of your emotional reactions and develop a greater sense of control over them. Techniques like meditation, deep breathing, and mindful walking can be particularly effective.

Set Healthy Boundaries
Establishing boundaries is crucial for maintaining your mental and emotional health. This means knowing when to say no, understanding your limits, and not allowing others to take advantage of you. Clear boundaries help you protect your energy and focus on what truly matters to you.

Cultivate Self-Awareness
Being self-aware means understanding your own emotions, triggers, and patterns of behavior. This awareness allows you to respond to situations thoughtfully instead of reacting impulsively. Journaling, therapy, and reflective practices can help you develop deeper self-awareness.

Let Go of the Need for Control
Understand that you cannot control everything, especially other people's actions and the outcomes of certain situations. Focus on what you can control—your own actions and responses. Accepting this can relieve a lot of stress and anxiety.

Focus on the Present
Often, we become attached to past events or future expectations. Practicing living in the present moment can help you appreciate life as it is and reduce unnecessary worry and regret. Engage fully in whatever you are doing right now, whether it's working, spending time with loved ones, or enjoying a hobby.

Develop Emotional Resilience
Emotional resilience is the ability to bounce back from setbacks and maintain a positive outlook. Building resilience involves maintaining a healthy lifestyle, nurturing supportive relationships, and practicing self-compassion. Resilient individuals tend to be better at detaching because they can see challenges as temporary and surmountable.

Embrace Change
Change is a constant part of life. Learning to accept and adapt to change can help you maintain a sense of stability and reduce attachment to specific outcomes. View change as an opportunity for growth and new experiences rather than a threat.

Find Your Inner Peace
Engage in activities that bring you joy and relaxation, such as hobbies, exercise, or spending time in nature. These activities can help you connect with your inner self and maintain a sense of peace regardless of external circumstances.

Seek Support When Needed
Detachment can be challenging, especially if you're dealing with difficult relationships or situations. Don't hesitate to seek support from friends, family, or a professional therapist that you trust. They can offer guidance, perspective, and encouragement.

By mastering the art of detachment, you can lead a more balanced, peaceful, and fulfilling life. Remember, detachment is not about withdrawing from life but engaging with it in a healthier, more sustainable way.

Chapter 17: Accepting What you Cannot Control

Accepting what you cannot control is an essential life skill that can lead to a more peaceful and fulfilling existence. This concept is often encapsulated in the Serenity Prayer, which asks for the serenity to accept the things we cannot change, the courage to change the things we can, and the wisdom to know the difference.

Why Acceptance is Important

Reduces Stress:
Constantly worrying about things beyond your control can lead to chronic stress and anxiety. Acceptance helps you let go of this unnecessary burden.

Improves Relationships:
Accepting others as they are—rather than trying to change them—can lead to more harmonious relationships.

Fosters Personal Growth:

Acceptance doesn't mean complacency. It means acknowledging reality so you can focus your energy on what you can change, thereby fostering personal growth.

Steps to Acceptance

Acknowledge Your Feelings:
The first step is recognizing and accepting your emotions. Whether it's frustration, sadness, or anger, acknowledging these feelings can help you process them.

Identify What You Can Control:
Make a list of things you can and cannot control. For example, you can control your reactions and efforts but not the outcomes or other people's actions.

Shift Your Focus:
Once you've identified what you can control, direct your energy and efforts toward these aspects. This shift in focus can be empowering and productive.

Practice Mindfulness:
Mindfulness techniques, such as meditation and deep breathing, can help you stay present and reduce the urge to control everything.

Seek Support:
Sometimes talking to a friend or a therapist that you trust can provide new perspectives and coping strategies for accepting what you cannot control.

Practical Tips

Limit Information Overload:

Constantly checking the news or social media can make you feel more out of control. Set boundaries for your media consumption.

Set Realistic Expectations:
Understand that not everything will go as planned. Set flexible goals that allow for unforeseen circumstances.

Focus on Your Response:
You can't control what happens, but you can control how you respond. Developing a positive and resilient mindset can make a big difference.

Accepting what you cannot control is not about giving up; it's about letting go of futile struggles to focus on what you can influence. This approach can lead to a more balanced, peaceful, and ultimately happier life. By practicing acceptance, you can navigate life's uncertainties with greater ease and grace.

18

Chapter 18: Legacy

Legacy is a powerful concept that encompasses the lasting impact individuals or groups leave behind after they are gone. It can manifest in various forms, including cultural, financial, intellectual, and ethical contributions. Legacy often reflects the values, achievements, and influence of a person or organization, shaping future generations and societal norms.

One of the most profound examples of legacy is in the realm of education. Some have left behind a wealth of knowledge and inspiration that continues to drive scientific discovery and innovation. Their legacies are not just measured by their discoveries but also by the countless minds they have inspired.

Their legacies are seen in the countless lives improved through their generosity and vision.

Cultural legacy is another significant aspect, where artists, musicians, writers, and filmmakers leave behind works that continue to influence and move people long after their creators are gone. These are timeless examples of how cultural contributions can become an enduring part of human history.

Ethical and moral legacies are often the most personal and intimate. These are the values and principles instilled in family members or followers.

In a more personal context, legacy can be the memories and values passed down within a family. It can be the traditions, stories, and lessons that parents and grandparents share with their children, shaping their worldview and character.

Ultimately, legacy is about the lasting footprint we leave on the world. It's a testament to our actions, choices, and the way we touch the lives of others. Building a meaningful legacy involves living with purpose, making a positive impact, and striving to leave the world a better place than we found it.

19

Chapter 19: Change

Change is an inevitable part of life. It can be daunting, exciting, and transformative all at once. Whether it's a change in our personal lives, careers, or even in society as a whole, embracing change can lead to growth and new opportunities.

In personal life, change might come in the form of moving to a new city, starting a new relationship, or embarking on a new educational journey. Each of these changes can bring about a mix of emotions, from fear and uncertainty to excitement and hope. The key to navigating personal change is to stay open-minded, adaptable, and resilient.

In the professional realm, change often means the advent of new technologies, shifts in industry standards, or transitions in entrepreneurial roles. Embracing change can lead to professional growth and new opportunities. It often requires continuous learning and the development of new skills. Staying proactive and being willing to step out of your comfort zone are crucial for thriving in a constantly evolving world.

Societal change, on the other hand, encompasses the broader shifts in cultural norms, values, and policies. These changes can be driven by movements for social justice, technological advancements, or significant events. Engaging with societal change requires awareness, empathy, and a willingness to be part of the conversation. It can lead to a more inclusive, equitable, and progressive society.

While change can be challenging, it is also a catalyst for progress. Embracing change allows us to adapt, grow, and ultimately become better versions of ourselves. It's important to remember that change is a natural part of life, and with the right mindset, it can be a powerful force for good.

20

Chapter 20: Complexion of Rejection

Rejection is an experience that everyone encounters at some point in their lives, and its impact can be profound and multifaceted. The "complexion of rejection" refers to the various ways in which rejection can manifest and affect us as individuals.

Emotional Impact

Rejection often triggers a cascade of emotions such as sadness, anger, confusion, and even self-doubt. It's common to feel hurt or to question one's self-worth after facing rejection, whether it's from a failed business endeavor, a romantic relationship, or a social group.

Psychological Consequences

On a deeper psychological level, rejection can lead to feelings of inadequacy and can affect one's mental health. It may contribute to anxiety, depression, or a diminished sense of self-esteem. Understanding that rejection is a normal part of life and not a reflection of one's inherent value is essential for maintaining mental well-being.

Social Dynamics

Socially, rejection can alter one's interactions and relationships. It may cause someone to withdraw from social situations or become more guarded in their interactions. Conversely, it can also foster resilience and a stronger sense of self when handled constructively.

Coping Mechanisms

Effective coping mechanisms are critical in managing the fallout from rejection. These can include:

Self-reflection:

Understanding why the rejection happened and what can be learned from the experience.

Support systems:

Relying on friends, family, or professional counselors that you trust to provide emotional support.

Positive activities:

Engaging in hobbies, exercise, or other activities that boost mood and confidence.

Growth and Resilience

While rejection is often painful, it can also be a powerful catalyst for growth and resilience. Facing and overcoming rejection can teach valuable lessons, build character, and lead to greater success in the future. It's important to reframe rejection not as a failure but as an opportunity for improvement and self-discovery.

The complexion of rejection is indeed complex, encompassing a wide range of emotional, psychological, social, and personal growth aspects.

By understanding and addressing the various facets of rejection, we can navigate these experiences more effectively and emerge stronger and more self-assured

A Letter to my Angel

Georgia Bernice Smith

When I lost you, I felt my entire world crumble. As I sit and reflect on the non-traumatic childhood memories, they all lead back to you. You were more than just the glue to our family; your smile will forever symbolize the most immaculate sunrise while your kisses displayed the most beautiful sunset that I will ever encounter.

Though this journey of mine seems to stretch far and wide with good times and bad, I have always felt your spirit and your presence. Even in your absence your guidance has never abandoned me.

With this dedication, I vow to carry on the beautiful legacy that you left behind for us here on earth.

I vow to always make you proud until we meet again.

Sincerely,

Your Whitney Houston

ACKNOWLEDGEMENTS

To my Manager, Luciano Layne

Wow! Thank you for everything! You are the perfect definition of an Angel here on Earth. They say that God's timing is always perfect and I for one am very grateful for all that you have contributed to my life, career and legacy.

I am truly humbled by the example that you have set for me in building my character and remaining relentless on this journey to my legacy.

Thank you for all the rooms that you have put me in and for being a vessel unto the Lord. I know that only God can do that. Continue serving and watch how God will continue to use men to bless you.

Sincerely,

Denise Smith

To my Coach, Joseph Pridgen

I wholeheartedly pray that God will bless you, your beautiful wife and everything attached to you in miraculous ways. Thank you for always accepting me and displaying the love of God in a very genuine way.

Just in case I never get another opportunity to give you your flowers, I'll use this one to express my gratitude.

Being under your mentorship and coaching program has contributed to my life in ways that you could never imagine and the spiritual connection is one that I will always hold dear to my heart.

To more success and life more abundantly.

Sincerely,

Denise Smith

To my Tribe,

There are no words that could express how grateful I am for such a strong support system. It is one that I never dreamed of having in my life. From the bottom of my heart I want to say thank you to each and every one of you who have contributed and had such a positive impact on my life. For all the times that you were there when I needed you the most I am so thankful.

Sincerely,

Denise Smith

DEDICATIONS

In Loving Memory of Travis Santanio Weaver

Travis was a highly spiritual person and always wanted to help his family. His biggest dream was to get all of his family back together and keep them together. He always kept his faith in God and his spirit will always be here with us. He was a loving, outgoing and multitalented person.

-Nicole Cline-Mull – Mother of Travis Weaver

Encouraging Words from the Author

In the midst of adversity, turmoil, rejection and pain there is always a light at the end of the tunnel. One day in the near future you will learn that life never really happened to you but it happened for you. It's never your past that defines and designs your future but the way that you perceive yourself, your life and your God given purpose will always determine your future. In learning to adapt you will learn to create and cultivate a beautiful life and legacy for yourself and your loved ones. Always speak abundance over yourself and everything attached to you and keep God first.
    -Denise Smith

www.ingramcontent.com/pod-product-compliance
Lightning Source LLC
LaVergne TN
LVHW051036070526
838201LV00010B/226